Lerner SPORTS™

SPORTS TEAM SMACKDOWN

SAN FRANCISCO 49ERS VS. LOS ANGELES RAMS

RIVAL RUMBLE

ABBY COLICH

Lerner Publications ◆ Minneapolis

Stats in this book are accurate through the 2024 National Football League season.

Lerner Publications Company
An imprint of Lerner Publishing Group, Inc.
241 First Avenue North
Minneapolis, MN 55401 USA

For reading levels and more information, look up this title at www.lernerbooks.com.

Main body text set in Aptifer Sans LT Pro. Typeface provided by Linotype AG.

Editor: Matt Doeden

Library of Congress Cataloging-in-Publication Data

Names: Colich, Abby, author.
Title: San Francisco 49ers vs. Los Angeles Rams : rival rumble / Abby Colich.
Other titles: San Francisco 49ers versus Los Angeles Rams
Description: Minneapolis, MN : Lerner Publications, [2026] | Series: Sports team smackdown (Lerner sports) | Includes bibliographical references and index. | Audience: Ages 7–11 | Audience: Grades 4–6 | Summary: "The rivalry between the San Francisco 49ers and Los Angeles Rams is about more than intrastate geography. Both NFL teams have experienced great success. But which team is best? Learn more and make your pick!"— Provided by publisher.
Identifiers: LCCN 2024050334 (print) | LCCN 2024050335 (ebook) | ISBN 9798765668665 (library binding) | ISBN 9798765683521 (paperback) | ISBN 9798765681695 (epub)
Subjects: LCSH: Sports rivalries—California—Juvenile literature. | San Francisco 49ers (Football team—Juvenile literature. | Los Angeles Rams (Football team : 2016–)—Juvenile literature.
Classification: LCC GV958.U518 C65 2026 (print) | LCC GV958.U518 (ebook) | DDC 796.332/640979461—dc23/eng/20250208

LC record available at https://lccn.loc.gov/2024050334
LC ebook record available at https://lccn.loc.gov/2024050335

Manufactured in the United States of America
1-1011976-53834-3/18/2025

TABLE OF CONTENTS

INTRODUCTION

A CHANCE AT THE SUPER BOWL

On January 30, 2022, the Los Angeles Rams played the San Francisco 49ers in the NFC Championship Game. The winner would go on to play in the Super Bowl.

The Rams had lost their last six games against the 49ers, a losing streak that reached back three seasons. And as the fourth quarter started, the Rams were down by 10. Los Angeles

Rams tight end Tyler Higbee (top right) takes a big hit in the NFC Championship Game on January 30, 2022.

quarterback Matthew Stafford spotted wide receiver Cooper Kupp running down the left side of the field. Stafford zipped a pass, and Kupp caught it for a touchdown.

Two fourth-quarter field goal kicks by Matt Gay gave the Rams a 20–17 lead. With just over a minute to go, the 49ers tried to come back. But Rams defender JaMycal Hasty intercepted a pass from 49ers quarterback Jimmy Garoppolo. The big win sent the Rams to the Super Bowl and snapped their losing streak against the 49ers.

FAST FACTS

- The Rams started in Cleveland, Ohio. They also played in St. Louis, Missouri.
- The San Francisco 49ers formed in 1946 as a part of the All-American Football Conference.
- In 1995, the 49ers became the first team to reach five Super Bowl wins. They also hold the National Football League (NFL) record for most playoff wins.
- When the Rams won the Super Bowl in 2022, they were only the second team to do so on their home field—SoFi Stadium.

This was just another exciting chapter in the rivalry between two California teams only 350 miles (560 km) apart. Their heated rivalry turns every season, every game, and every play between these two powerhouses into an all-out battle. But which team is the best? Read on and decide for yourself. Who is the champion of this rival smackdown?

Rams receiver Odell Beckham Jr. catches a pass in the NFC Championship Game.

SMACKDOWN!

CHAPTER 1

49ers defenders close in on Rams receiver Elroy Hirsch (center) in this 1950 game.

TWO CALIFORNIA TEAMS

The San Francisco 49ers formed in 1946 as a part of the All-American Football Conference. In 1950, the 49ers joined the NFL. From 1950 to 1969, the 49ers made it to the playoffs only once. They lost to the Detroit Lions in the first round in 1957.

The 49ers won their division in 1970 and 1971 but lost to the Dallas Cowboys in the conference championship both years. Quarterback Joe Montana joined the 49ers in 1979. He helped the team win Super Bowls in 1982, 1985, 1989, and 1990.

With another Super Bowl win in 1995, the 49ers became the first team to win the title five times. They beat the San Diego Chargers 49–26. The 49ers made it back to the Super Bowl in 2013, 2020, and 2024, but lost all three times.

49ers quarterback Joe Montana runs to avoid Cincinnati Bengals defenders in the Super Bowl on January 24, 1982.

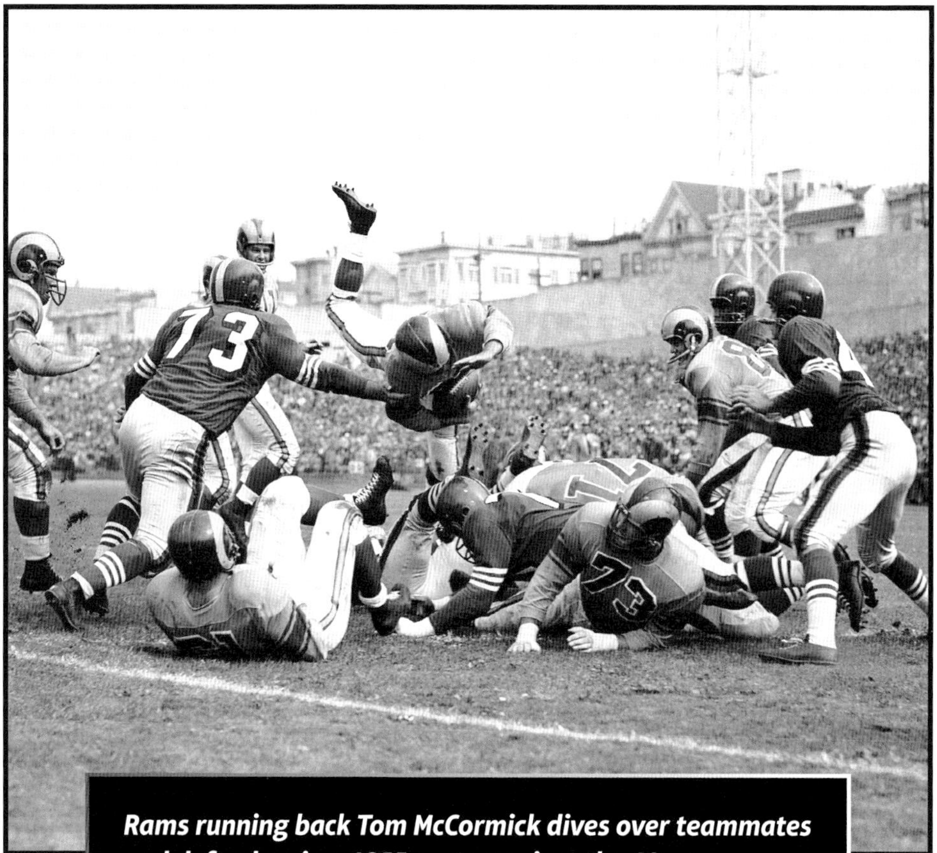

Rams running back Tom McCormick dives over teammates and defenders in a 1955 game against the 49ers.

The Rams formed in Cleveland in 1936. In 1945, they had their first winning record and ended the season with the NFL Championship. The next year, the Rams moved to Los Angeles, California. In 1951, the team won another title, beating the Cleveland Browns 24–17.

The Rams made it to the playoffs every year from 1973 to 1980. They reached their first Super Bowl after the 1979 season but lost to the Pittsburgh Steelers.

In 1995, the team moved to St Louis. Four years later, quarterback Kurt Warner led them to a record of 13 wins and 3 losses. They beat the Tennessee Titans in the Super Bowl 23–16. They returned to the Super Bowl in 2002 but lost to the New England Patriots.

CHECK IT OUT

The 1995 Super Bowl was the highest scoring Super Bowl of all time. The 49ers beat the San Diego Chargers 49–26. The 49ers also hold the record for most points scored in a Super Bowl with 55 in 1990.

Quarterback Kurt Warner leads the Rams to a Super Bowl victory on January 30, 2000.

In 2016, the Rams moved back to Los Angeles. Head coach Sean McVay led them to the Super Bowl in 2022. They played on their home field to beat the Cincinnati Bengals 23–20. That made the Rams just the second team to win the title on their own field.

The rivalry between the Rams and 49ers goes back to 1950. The Rams won their first matchup 35–14. The teams have played each other every year since.

Rams quarterback Jim Everett tries to hide the ball from the 49ers defense during the 1990 NFC Championship Game.

Wide receiver Deebo Samuel slices through the Rams defense in the NFC Championship Game in 2022.

Both teams have had long winning streaks in the rivalry. The Rams won 10 straight games from 1970 to 1975. The 49ers won 17 straight meetings during the 1990s.

The 49ers and Rams have only met twice in the playoffs. Both times were NFC Championship Games. The 49ers beat the Rams 30–3 in 1990. The Rams beat the 49ers 20–17 in 2022.

CHAPTER 2

49ers receiver Dwight Clark spikes the ball after scoring the game-winning touchdown in the NFC Championship Game on January 10, 1982.

MANY GREAT MOMENTS

Both the 49ers and Rams give their fans thrilling moments every season.

In 1982, the 49ers trailed the Dallas Cowboys by six points in the playoffs. With less than a minute left, 49ers receiver Dwight Clark caught a pass from Joe Montana in the end zone to win the game. The 49ers went on to win their first Super Bowl.

The 49ers faced the Green Bay Packers in the 1999 playoffs. With two minutes left, the Packers scored a touchdown to take a 27–23 lead. With the ball back, the 49ers moved down the field to the 25-yard line. Quarterback Steve Young threw the ball to Terrell Owens, who caught it in the end zone with three seconds left. The 49ers won 30–27.

In the final four minutes of their 2012 playoff game, the 49ers exchanged the lead with the New Orleans Saints four times. With 14 seconds left, 49ers quarterback Alex Smith threw a pass to tight end Vernon Davis for a touchdown. The 49ers won 36–32.

Receiver Terrell Owens pulls in a tough catch to help the 49ers beat the Packers on January 3, 1999.

In the fourth quarter of their 1979 NFC playoff game, the Rams trailed the Cowboys by five points with about two minutes to go. Rams quarterback Vince Ferragamo passed the ball to receiver Billy Waddy, who sprinted down the field for a 50-yard touchdown. The Rams went on to win the game but later lost in the Super Bowl.

Late in the 2000 Super Bowl, quarterback Kurt Warner threw a 73-yard pass to Isaac Bruce for the lead. The Titans drove down the field, hoping to score a game-tying

Kurt Warner had a late start to his career. He didn't play in the NFL until the age of 27.

Rams linebacker Mike Jones makes a game-saving tackle of Titans receiver Kevin Dyson in the Super Bowl.

touchdown. But Rams linebacker Mike Jones tackled Titans receiver Kevin Dyson at the 1-yard line as the clock hit zero. The Rams won 23–16.

After losing the 2019 Super Bowl, the Rams reached the big game again in 2022. They trailed the Bengals by four points. With a little more than a minute left, quarterback Matthew Stafford threw a touchdown pass to Cooper Kupp. The Rams won 23–20.

The 49ers and Rams rivalry has been exciting from the beginning. Their first game on October 1, 1950, included a 97-yard kickoff return touchdown from Vitamin Smith to put the Rams ahead. They went on to win the game 35–14.

The Rams' 2017 season was their first after moving back to Los Angeles. And their week 3 game against the 49ers meant the return of the Battle of California. The Rams led the entire game. The 49ers tried to keep up, but they missed a two-point conversion for a tie late in the game. The Rams won 41–39.

The Rams and 49ers meet for the first time on October 1, 1950.

49ers kicker Robbie Gould kicks a game-winning field goal against the Rams in 2019.

For a chance at the playoffs, the Rams needed a win in week 16 of the 2019 season. With less than three minutes left in the fourth quarter, they kicked a field goal to tie the 49ers 31–31. But 49ers kicker Robbie Gould dashed their hopes with a short field goal as time ran out.

CHECK IT OUT

Marshall Faulk, Kurt Warner, Isaac Bruce, and Torry Holt were part of The Greatest Show on Turf from 1999 to 2001. They helped the Rams become the first NFL team to score a total of 500 points over three seasons.

CHAPTER 3

Quarterback Joe Montana led the 49ers to greatness in the 1980s.

POWERFUL PLAYERS

One of the greatest NFL quarterbacks of all time, Joe Montana, played for the 49ers from 1979 to 1992. The Comeback Kid helped his team come from behind to win in the fourth quarter 31 times. He won four Super Bowls with the 49ers and was named Super Bowl MVP three times.

On the defensive side, Ronnie Lott played safety for the 49ers from 1981 to 1990. In 20 playoff games for the team, he had nine interceptions. He returned two of them for touchdowns.

Jerry Rice was a wide receiver for the 49ers from 1985 to 2000. During that time, he broke many receiving records. He scored 208 touchdowns during his career, the most in NFL history.

Steve Young was the quarterback of the 49ers from 1987 to 1999. His biggest game was the 1995 Super Bowl. He threw a Super Bowl record six touchdown passes, leading his team to victory.

Many fans and experts call Jerry Rice the greatest wide receiver in NFL history.

Terrell Owens played for the 49ers from 1996 to 2003. The wide receiver caught a record 20 passes in a single game against the Chicago Bears in 2000.

Running back Eric Dickerson played for the Rams from 1983 to 1987. He holds the NFL record for most rushing yards in a season at 2,105. He also had the most rushing yards in a playoff game at 248.

Quarterback Kurt Warner was a surprise star for the Rams. He had been working at a grocery store before he joined the Rams in 1998. Warner set a Super Bowl record in 2000 with 414 passing yards. His record stood for 18 years before it was broken by Tom Brady in 2017.

Quarterback Kurt Warner calls out signals before a play in 1999.

Rams defensive tackle Aaron Donald (left) was one of the most dominant defenders in the league from 2014 to 2023.

During his time as a Ram from 1999 to 2006, running back Marshall Faulk was named NFL Offensive Player of the Year three times. He helped take the team to their first Super Bowl and still holds the Rams all-time touchdown record with 85.

A Ram from 2014 to 2023, Aaron Donald was one of the greatest defensive players of all time. He holds the team record for most sacks at 111.

Wide receiver Cooper Kupp joined the Rams in 2017. He helped lead the team to their Super Bowl win in 2022. That year, he broke an NFL record for regular season and playoff receiving yards with 2,425.

CHECK IT OUT

Rosie Grier, Lamar Lundy, Merlin Olsen, and Deacon Jones were part of the Rams defensive starting line in the 1960s. They were called the Fearsome Foursome. From 1964 to 1968, the Rams defense allowed the fewest rushing yards in the NFL.

Rams receiver Cooper Kupp fights off a 49ers tackler in 2022.

CHAPTER 4

Rams running back Kyren Williams (right) takes a handoff in a 2024 game against the 49ers.

CHOOSE YOUR CHAMPION

Do you like to compare your favorite team against their rivals? Let's take a look at how the 49ers and Rams compare.

The 49ers have won more of their games. The 49ers have won 53.9 percent of all their games. The Rams have won 50.6 percent of their games. The 49ers have won more Super Bowls. They won five while the Rams have only won two.

The 49ers lead the series rivalry. They won 53 percent of all games the teams have played against each other. Therefore, the edge goes to the 49ers!

Now it's your turn. Who do you think wins this football smackdown?

A pair of 49ers defenders sacks Rams quarterback Matthew Stafford in 2024.

49ers quarterback Brock Purdy runs in the rain as a Rams defender closes in to make the tackle.

SMACKDOWN TIMELINE

SAN FRANCISCO 49ERS

1946 The 49ers form as a part of the All-American Football Conference.

1950 The 49ers join the NFL.

1979 The 49ers draft quarterback Joe Montana.

1982 The 49ers beat the Cincinnati Bengals to win their first Super Bowl.

1985 The 49ers beat the Miami Dolphins in the Super Bowl 38–16.

1989 The 49ers come from behind to beat the Bengals in the Super Bowl 20–16.

1990 The 49ers score the most points ever in a Super Bowl. They beat the Denver Broncos 55–10.

2024 The 49ers play in their ninth Super Bowl. They lose to the Kansas City Chiefs 25–22 in overtime.

LOS ANGELES RAMS

1936 The Rams form in Cleveland.

1945 The Rams win their first NFL Championship.

1946 The Rams move to Los Angeles.

1951 The Rams beat the Cleveland Browns, winning another NFL Championship.

1980 The Rams make it to the Super Bowl for the first time. They lose to the Pittsburgh Steelers.

1994 The Rams move to St Louis.

2000 The Rams win their first Super Bowl. They beat the Tennessee Titans 23–16.

2016 The Rams move back to Los Angeles.

2022 The Rams beat the Cincinnati Bengals to win their second Super Bowl.

GLOSSARY

division: a group of teams that directly compete against one another

drive: a series of football plays

end zone: the area on a football field beyond the goal line where points are scored

interception: when a pass is caught by the defense

MVP: most valuable player

NFC: National Football Conference, one of two groups of teams in the NFL

NFL Championship: the game that determined the NFL's champion before the Super Bowl era

rivalry: fierce competition between two teams

sack: to tackle the quarterback for a loss of yards

safety: a defensive player whose job it is to make tackles and prevent big plays

two-point conversion: advancing the ball across the goal line by running or catching a pass after a touchdown

LEARN MORE

Anderson, Josh. *Inside the Los Angeles Rams*. Lerner Publications, 2024.

Britannica Kids: Los Angeles Rams
https://kids.britannica.com/students/article/Los-Angeles-Rams/571026

Pro Football Hall of Fame: Los Angeles Rams
https://www.profootballhof.com/teams/los-angeles-rams/

Pro Football Hall of Fame: San Francisco 49ers
https://www.profootballhof.com/teams/san-francisco-49ers/

Scheffer, Janie. *The San Francisco 49ers*. Bellwether Media, 2024.

Whiting, Jim. *The Story of the Los Angeles Rams*. Creative Education, Creative Paperbacks, 2025.

INDEX

PHOTO ACKNOWLEDGMENTS

Image credits: AP Photo/Michael Owens, pp. 4, 7 (bottom); AP Photo/Icon Sportswire, p. 6; AP Photo/Ben Liebenberg, pp. 7 (top), 23; AP Photo/Vic Stein, pp. 8, 18; AP Photo/Al Messerschmidt, pp. 9, 11, 22; AP Photo/RHH, p. 10; AP Photo/Al Golub, p. 12; AP Photo/John McGillen, p. 13; AP Photo/Peter Read Miller, p. 14; AP Photo/Susan Ragan, p. 15; AP Photo/Carlos Osorio, p. 16; AP Photo/Michael Conroy, p. 17; Lachlan Cunningham/Getty Images, p. 19; AP Photo/Paul Spinelli, p. 20; AP Photo/Joe Pugli, p. 21; AP Photo/Marcio Jose Sanchez, p. 24; Ezra Shaw/Getty Images, p. 25; AP Photo/Jed Jacobsohn, p. 26; AP Photo/Godofredo A. Vásquez, p. 27. Design elements: Trisno Wardana/Shutterstock; Ihor Biliavskyi/Shutterstock; Joko Ribowo/Shutterstock.

Cover: AP Photo/Eakin Howard; AP Photo/Kevin Terrell.